He Said Yes

*The Story of
Father Mychal Judge*

by Kelly Ann Lynch

ILLUSTRATIONS BY
M. Scott Oatman

Paulist Press
New York/Mahwah, NJ

Caseside design by Lynn Else
Caseside illustration by M. Scott Oatman

Text Copyright © 2007 by Kelly Ann Lynch
Illustrations Copyright © 2007 by M. Scott Oatman

Library of Congress Cataloging-in-Publication Data

Lynch, Kelly Ann.
    He said yes : the story of Father Mychal Judge / by Kelly Ann Lynch;
    illustrations by M. Scott Oatman.
        p. cm.
    ISBN 978-0-8091-6740-1 (alk. paper)
    1. Judge, Mychal, 1933–2001—Juvenile literature. 2. September 11 Terrorist Attacks, 2001—Biography—Juvenile literature. 3. Catholic Church—United States—Clergy—Biography—Juvenile literature.
I. Oatman, M. Scott. II. Title.
    BX4705.J767L96 2007
    282.092—dc22
    [B]
                                                                                        2007000049

Published by Paulist Press
997 Macarthur Boulevard
Mahwah, New Jersey 07430

www.paulistpress.com

Printed and bound in the United States of America

To the Holy Spirit, who inspired me to write this story.
To my husband, my children, and my parents,
who continue to inspire me every day.
To Father Mychal, who taught me to say yes.
And to all those I've met while walking in his footsteps.
K.A.L.

To my family—
Thank you for all of your love and support.
To Father Mychal—
I never imagined my life could be so greatly affected
by someone I never met.
M.S.O.

It was a warm, sunny day in Brooklyn, New York, in May of 1933, when Robert Emmet Judge began his life on earth. His parents, Michael Judge and Mary Fallon Judge, were from Ireland and had settled in Brooklyn before he was born. His family called him Emmet. He had a twin sister named Dympna and an older sister named Erin.

Emmet was only six years old when his father died. Emmet was sad and wanted to help his mother, so he did odd jobs around the house and ran errands for her. He was always looking for ways to make extra money to help his family, so when he was asked to go to work shining shoes,

he said yes.

One day, on his way to shine shoes, Emmet passed by St. Francis of Assisi Church on West 31st Street in Manhattan. He felt drawn to stop and go inside. The sun shined through the beautiful stained-glass windows of the church, and Emmet felt the presence of God through the friars. These friars were Franciscan priests and brothers who wore brown robes and sandals. They followed Jesus like St. Francis did long ago. Their simple belt was made of rope, and it was knotted three times. This represented the three vows they had taken—poverty, chastity, and obedience.

One particular friar noticed Emmet and welcomed him into this house of God. Emmet followed the friar all around the church, and learned that friars live out the gospel of Jesus in a simple way. Emmet knew then that he wanted to live out the gospel too. He wanted to wear the robe of a Franciscan and become a friar.

As a teenager, he began visiting the church regularly and often thought about becoming a priest. When he felt called to finish high school at a seminary,

he said yes.

Each day at the seminary, in addition to his schoolwork, Emmet attended daily Mass, cleaned his room, and shared meals with his friends. The Franciscan priests and brothers took good care of him and taught him many things. Emmet learned that St. Francis had said yes when he was asked by God to follow him.

Emmet also learned that St. Francis was once a rich man who gave away everything he had and lived among the poor. St. Francis wanted to share God's love with everyone. Emmet knew that he wanted to live like St. Francis and share God's love with everyone too.

Emmet graduated high school. A few years later, when he felt that he was being called to follow in the footsteps of St. Francis,

he said yes.

This was the beginning of a new life for Emmet. His dream of following St. Francis was now a reality. How happy he was when the Franciscan priests and brothers welcomed him by giving him his own special brown robe and sandals. Later, when he became a priest, he would sometimes have to wear black clothes and a white collar. But he always loved his brown robe the best.

As a Franciscan brother, Emmet was invited to choose a new name to go along with this new beginning. In honor of his mother and father, he chose the name Fallon Michael, then changed it to Michael Fallon. He later changed the spelling of Michael to M-Y-C-H-A-L because so many friars had chosen the same name. From then on, everyone knew Emmet as Mychal.

Mychal continued his studies to become a Franciscan priest. Ever since he was a little boy in Brooklyn, this had been his dream.

Finally, after years of study, when Mychal was asked to profess his final vows and to become a priest,

he said yes.

Everyone now called him Father Mychal. He could celebrate Mass, hear confessions, preach the gospel, perform weddings and baptisms, and bury the dead. Father Mychal was sent to work in many different churches in Massachusetts and New Jersey, and finally back in New York, in the same church he had been drawn to as a child.

Just like Jesus, Saint Francis loved taking care of the poor and the sick. And so did Father Mychal. One of the ways he could do this was by giving food to people who came to the breadline at St. Francis Church. There the friars had been feeding the homeless and the hungry for many years, even before Father Mychal was born.

Each morning many people would come to the breadline to eat. These were people who had no home and had to sleep in cardboard boxes on the sidewalk or in doorways at night. They had no food and were hungry. But thanks to the friars and the breadline, they could start each day with a meal.

Father Mychal knew he had to help these people, and so when they asked him for something to eat and drink,

he said yes.

Father Mychal was happy to be back in New York City. He loved the city. He loved the people who lived there. And he loved to walk.

One day, Father Mychal walked from St. Francis of Assisi Church, down many city blocks, across the Brooklyn Bridge, and all the way to Coney Island. It was a very long walk, but a friend went with him. When they got to Coney Island, they sat, talked, and enjoyed ice-cream cones together.

The Brooklyn Bridge was one of Father Mychal's favorite places to walk. He always got ideas on the bridge, ideas about how he could help more people. One day, he stopped on the bridge and looked at the city. He thanked God for allowing him to become a priest. And when the city seemed to call out to him to bless it,

he said yes.

Father Mychal tried to be kind to everyone. He believed that all people were created by God and deserved God's mercy and love.

One day, he heard about a man who was dying from a serious illness. Many people would not touch this man for fear of catching his disease, but Father Mychal was not afraid. He remembered how Jesus, and also St. Francis, helped the sick and dying when other people had turned their backs on them.

Father Mychal knew that this man would not live much longer and that he needed to feel the love of God. Father Mychal decided to bring the man a teddy bear so he had something to hold onto when he was all alone. And when the man silently asked Father Mychal for company and comfort,

he said yes.

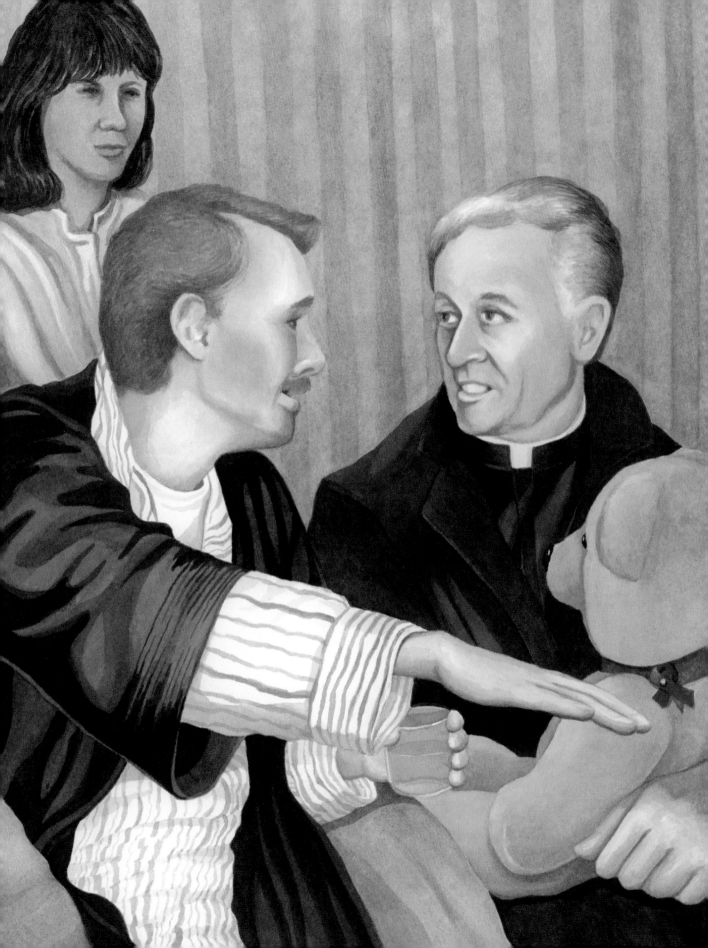

One of Father Mychal's friends gave birth to a baby girl. The baby was very sick. Doctors needed to give the baby part of her mother's liver in an operation to make her well again. On a cold winter day before the baby's surgery, Father Mychal went to his friend's home and prayed with her family. It had been snowing outside and there was a chill in the air, but Father Mychal arrived in his brown robe and sandals just the same. How he loved being a Franciscan!

The family gathered together and held hands as Father Mychal gave them strength. He reminded them that God was always with them and that they shouldn't worry about the future. "Don't worry about tomorrow," he told them, "for God hasn't even created it yet."

When he was asked to bless the baby and to be with the family during such a difficult time,

he said yes.

Ever since Father Mychal was a small boy in Brooklyn, he loved fire engines. When he heard the sirens, he would always run to the window to see the bright red fire trucks racing down his street. He often wondered what it would be like to be a fireman.

Father Mychal was always looking for more ways to help people, so when he was asked to go to work as a chaplain for the New York City Fire Department,

he said yes.

Father Mychal knew how important prayer was and could often be found on his knees praying to God. He believed that God listened to all prayers. So Father Mychal prayed every day for the many people he knew and loved.

One day, Father Mychal heard about a police detective in the city who had been badly hurt. He knew that Cardinal O'Connor had been visiting and praying with the detective since the day of his injury. Father Mychal wanted to pray with him too. The detective was in a wheelchair and could no longer walk. His family was very sad. With the help of Cardinal O'Connor, Father Mychal, and other priests and friends, the detective forgave the man who hurt him. This brought peace to the detective's family. Through the years, Father Mychal became close friends with the detective and his wife and son.

Years later, the detective wanted to go to Ireland, where there was much fighting. He wanted to share his story in the hope of teaching people to forgive each other. He wanted to visit the prime minister, sign his name in the guestbook, and talk about peace. And when the detective's family asked Father Mychal to go to Ireland with them,

he said yes.

Father Mychal always hurried off to help people who needed him. Before leaving, he would pray to God in these words:

Lord, take me where you want me to go.
Let me meet who you want me to meet.
Tell me what you want me to say.
And keep me out of your way.

One day, a plane crashed into the water near Long Island, and many people died. When Father Mychal heard about this, he knew he needed to go to their families and be with them. He needed to tell them that their relatives and friends on the plane now looked down and could feel their love. His words gave comfort to the people that day.

When he felt called to go and pray with these families,

he said yes.

Life isn't always easy and no one is perfect. But Father Mychal believed we could all learn from our mistakes. "Life is a learning process," he often told his friends. Still, it's hard to learn, and some people learn slowly.

Father Mychal knew that some people couldn't drink alcohol. Whenever they drank it, they got sick. They had to learn to stop drinking alcohol, but it was very difficult to stop. They could go to meetings and talk to people who could help them. But even after they stopped drinking, they faced a long, hard road ahead.

At a meeting, Father Mychal met a young man whose parents had both died. The young man was sad and had been drinking too much alcohol. He needed to learn how to stop and to get well again. When the young man asked Father Mychal for help,

he said yes.

The skies were blue and the sun was shining on September 11, 2001, when airplanes crashed into the two towers of the World Trade Center in New York City. As soon as Father Mychal heard the news, he knew that he had to help the people who were hurt.

With a rosary in his hands, he raced to the scene. The mayor of the city was there. He reached out as Father Mychal was rushing toward the towers. "Pray for us, Father," the mayor said. "I always do," Father Mychal told him.

Many people ran away from the fire and smoke that morning, but Father Mychal did not. Like the firefighters he knew, Father Mychal was willing to risk his life to save others in a time of danger.

When Father Mychal ran to the towers, he was following in the footsteps of Jesus, who told his disciples, "No one has greater love than this, to lay down one's life for one's friends." Father Mychal lived and died by those words.

He said yes.

Can You Find Them All?

M. Scott Oatman, the man who painted this book, also painted tiny pictures right into many of the bigger pictures. In other words, he hid them! (If you want to see more of his artwork, visit him online at www.mscottoatman.com.)

Some of these hidden images will be easy to spot, others will be much harder. Every hidden image has to do with different events in Father Mychal's life. See if you can find all of them. The page number for each is given below.

5. A dove on the building beneath the left-most American flag
7. The Franciscan rope belt with three knots, on the tan building left of the church
9. A tau cross (find a picture of it online), and a book about St. Francis
11. The name Mychal in the shadow at Fr. Mychal's feet
13. The year the breadline began
15. Two ice-cream cones
17. The Christian symbol of a fish on the patient's bathrobe
19. 9/11
21. The number of firemen lost on 9/11
23. The Irish flag on a book titled *Peace in Ireland*
25. The number of people lost on TWA flight 800
27. Twelve Steps (of AA)
29. The twin towers of the World Trade Center, and the digits 0001 (the number on Father Mychal's death certificate)

Did you miss any? Kelly Ann Lynch, the author, has listed the answers on her Web site for Mychal's Message at www.mychalsmessage.org. There is more information about Mychal's Message on the next page.

Mychal's Message is a nonprofit organization dedicated to continuing the work of Father Mychal F. Judge, OFM, by meeting the needs of the homeless and sharing his message of unconditional love. Through our efforts, we hope to inspire others to do the same.

Mychal's Message began when eleven-year-old Shannon Hickey decided to collect socks for the homeless in memory of Father Mychal, who had died just four months earlier. Shannon Hickey is the daughter of the author and is also the baby in this story who received the living-donor liver transplant. The Lynches, the author's family counted Father Mychal as a dear friend, so everyone helped, and the socks were distributed to the homeless near Ground Zero in New York City.

From a child's simple gift of socks, Mychal's Message was born. In just its first few years, the organization collected and distributed to the homeless and poor the following items—

18,380 baby diapers

15,000 prayer cards

12,000 personal-size toiletries

10,000 items for a Philadelphia soup kitchen

8,430 pairs of underpants

6,783 pairs of socks

4,154 undershirts

1,606 hats, scarves, and gloves

1,122 pairs of new sneakers

—and literally tens of thousands of other items, from teddy bears to umbrellas, and everything in between.

Proceeds from this book will directly benefit the homeless.

Mychal's Message
P.O. Box 6404
Lancaster, PA 17607
www.mychalsmessage.org

Mychal's Prayer

Lord, take me where you want me to go.
Let me meet who you want me to meet.
Tell me what you want me to say.
And keep me out of your way.